THE ARCHITECTURE OF LUIS BARRAGAN

THE ARCHITECTURE OF LUIS BARRAGAN

Emilio Ambasz

The Museum of Modern Art, New York

Copyright © 1976 by The Museum of Modern Art
Fifth printing 1989
All rights reserved
Library of Congress Catalog Card Number 74-21724
Clothbound ISBN 0-87070-234-3
Paperbound ISBN 0-87070-233-5
Designed by Emilio Ambasz
Graphics Associate: Michael Lauretano
Typeset by Bullard/Morris & Walsh, Inc., New York
Printed by Colorcraft Lithographers, Inc., New York
Bound by Sendor Bindery, Inc., New York
The Museum of Modern Art
11 West 53 Street, New York, N.Y. 10019
Printed in the United States of America

Preface

Mexican-born Luis Barragán is one of landscape architecture's most refined and poetic practitioners. In the de Chirico-like settings he creates, the wall is both the supreme entity and the inhabitant of a larger metaphysical landscape, a screen for revealing the hidden colors of Mexico's almost white sun and a shield for suggesting never seen presences. His magnificent fountains and carefully constructed plazas seem to stand as great architectural stages for the promenade of mythological beings. While his design approach is classical and atemporal, the elements of his architecture are deeply rooted in his country's cultural and religious traditions. It is through the haunting beauty of his hieratic constructions that we have come to conceive of the passions of Mexico's architecture.

Although Barragán, now 74, has been justly admired through many magazine articles, this is the first book to be published on his work. The photographs that follow illustrate seven of Barragán's most accomplished projects, tracing the evolution and lyrical refinement of his work since the gardens of El Pedregal and his own house, which were among his first original architectural statements in the 40s. In addition, Barragán's *oeuvre* since 1927—including early projects evidencing strong influences from the Mediterranean and Le Corbusier's architecture, as well as unrealized projects of the last decade—is detailed in a List of Works at the end of the book.

On behalf of the Trustees of The Museum of Modern Art, I wish to express our indebtedness to Don Luis Barragán for giving us the opportunity of presenting his work and the pleasure of honoring his artistic achievements. I am particularly grateful to him for allowing me to roam freely in his house and studio, browsing among his books, opening drawers, and releasing many memories. I shall always cherish our conversations on architecture and on Mexico, instances of which are quoted in the following pages.

The Museum is most grateful to the National Endowment for the Arts, and to the Director of its Architecture and Environmental Arts Program, Mr. Bill Lacy, for having supported this project and the ensuing traveling exhibition.

Our heartfelt admiration and thanks go to Don Armando Salas Portugal, the great photographer of Mexico's landscape and architecture, who, for more than a quarter century has photographed Barragán's work. It is through his beautiful photographic compositions that we have been given the unique opportunity of studying the main body of Barragán's work. I am obliged to Miss Carla de Benedetti, of Milan, for making available to us her splendid photographs of the Egerstrom stables. I am particularly grateful to Rene Burri, of Zurich, whose exquisitely rendered photographs have allowed us to complement this book's documentation.

I am indebted in many ways to numerous members of the Museum staff, not least to John Limpert, Director of Membership and Development, for his enthusiastic support of this book. Richard Palmer, Coordinator of Exhibitions, has most ably supervised all administrative aspects. I wish to express my thanks to Michael Lauretano to whom I owe deep gratitude for his solicitous attention to this publication's design. To Patricia White, who served as editor, I am grateful alike for her subtlety and her enthusiasm for the task.

Within my own Department of Architecture and Design, I am especially grateful to its Director, Arthur Drexler, who encouraged me to undertake this project. I also wish to thank Ludwig Glaeser, Curator of the Mies van der Rohe Archive, for his generous cooperation. Mary Jane Lightbown provided invaluable assistance, and my secretary, Marie-Anne Evans, very competently helped in all matters related to this publication. To all of them I owe a debt of gratitude. —E. A.

Contents

"My house is my refuge, an emotional piece of architecture, not a cold piece of convenience."

"I believe in an 'emotional architecture.' It is very important for human kind that architecture should move by its beauty; if there are many equally valid technical solutions to a problem, the one which offers the user a message of beauty and emotion, that one is architecture."

"Any work of architecture which does not express serenity is a mistake. That is why it has been an error to replace the protection of walls with today's intemperate use of enormous glass windows."

"The construction and enjoyment of a garden accustoms people to beauty, to its instinctive use, even to its pursuit."

"I believe that architects should design gardens to be used, as much as the houses they build, to develop a sense of beauty and the taste and inclination toward the fine arts and other spiritual values."

—Luis Barragán

"My earliest childhood memories are related to a ranch my family owned near the village of Mazamitla. It was a *pueblo* with hills, formed by houses with tile roofs and immense eaves to shield passersby from the heavy rains which fall in that area. Even the earth's color was interesting because it was red earth. In this village, the water distribution system consisted of great gutted logs, in the form of troughs, which ran on a support structure of tree forks, 5 meters high, above the roofs. This aqueduct crossed over the town, reaching the patios, where there were great stone fountains to receive the water. The patios housed the stables, with cows and chickens, all together. Outside, in the street, there were iron rings to tie the horses. The channeled logs, covered with moss, dripped water all over town, of course. It gave this village the ambience of a fairy tale."

"No, there are no photographs. I have only its memory."

—Luis Barragán, extracted from conversations
with Emilio Ambasz

El Pedregal (The Rocky Place), formally known as
Parque Residencial Jardines del Pedregal de San Angel,
Periphery of Mexico, D.F. 1945–1950

The story of El Pedregal's birth and rebirth belongs with the innumerable legends of Mexico's creation. It first came into being approximately 2,500 years ago, when the Xitle volcano erupted in great lava waves which solidified into 15 square miles of convoluted crevices and caves. Over the centuries its core became a citadel of reptiles, scorpions and wild plants, while its edges provided the purplish gray lava rock used in many Toltec and Aztec constructions.

In 1944, Barragán bought a piece of land, called El Cabrío (the goat's pen), facing El Pedregal. It was a marvelous terrain, populated by big evergreen oaks and bordering on the river La Magdalena. A few of El Pedregal's rocky fingers reached into the land, rising 20 feet against the background of trees. By that time Barragán, who had produced several buildings for real estate clients in Guadalajara and Mexico City, had decided to retire completely from construction, disappointed with the restrictions Mexico City's speculative climate imposed upon his work. His purpose in acquiring El Cabrío was to create a complex of small, successive garden spaces where he could retire from time to time to meditate and enjoy nature (three private gardens, page 116). Prior to this purchase he had already been carrying home fantastic lava fragments to decorate the four contiguous gardens he was creating in the Tacubaya section of Mexico City, one of which later became part of his Mexico City house (four private gardens, page 116). Seduced by the savage beauty of its strange vegetation and the ominous shapes of its lava formations, Barragán began to evolve the idea, already anticipated in an essay by the painter Diego Rivera, of transforming the inhospitable El Pedregal into a livable garden, where Man and Nature could become reconciled. He felt it was a holy mission.

Barragán's plan was to create a residential area, respectful of both the existing lava formations and the extraordinary natural vegetation. Rather than houses, Barragán had in mind perhaps a vision closer to the ancient Persian concept of living quarters: he conceived of the garden as the soul of the house—the place where guests are received. He perceived of rooms as simple retreats meant just for sleeping, the storage of belongings, and shelter from hostile weather.

Seconded in his plans by the partnership of an able and courageous realtor, José Alberto Bustamante, they both acquired very inexpensively 865 acres of El Pedregal. The streets of the subdivision were so laid out that they followed within its crevices the natural contours of the lava formations. The contrasts were violent, but all parts maintained their separate integrities. At first, prospective clients shied away, fearful of snakes and cutting stone edges. To demonstrate the feasibility of his ideas, Barragán created three showpiece gardens (pages 16–21), bringing in topsoil and using the native Pedregal cacti, wild flowers, graceful pepper trees, and gnarled *palo bobo* (crazy tree). Steps and pathways were carved into the rocks; water pools and stone walls were disposed in such a seemingly effortless manner that the gardens seemed to have been born together with the sea of lava.

To define entrances to the subdivision, Barragán opened the walls here and there with fences of tall iron pickets painted phosphorescent reds and greens, and built decorative fountains and plazas (pages 22–25). The main entrance to the subdivision (Plaza de las Fuentes) presented several such fountains. The one known as Fuente de los Patos (Ducks' Fountain, page 20) used staggered lava walls to frame inner views complemented by a brimming pool and water entering from an unexpected source. Another fountain contrasted a low row of iron spikes with an intermittent jet, playing sensually with the ambiguities between verticals of soft and hard matter (page 13).

Barragán's vision called for the metamorphosis of the lava desert into a new configuration. The forms sheltering the houses were to emerge from the substance of the land (pages 14–15). A rigorous set of building restrictions was imposed upon construction and landscaping to obtain architectural harmony. The minimum lot size allowed was about one acre; the house could not occupy more than 10 per cent of the lot, the rest was to remain free space. The lava was to be protected, and the natural vegetation preserved. Any new planting was required to follow the contours, and any new construction had to be subordinated to the rock.

All houses were to be contemporary in design—the colonial style was expressly forbidden. The houses were to be surrounded by high lava rock walls. In this manner, Barragán paid his respects to the traditional Mexican home, which emphasized living in patios, behind walls. As each plot was to become a room open to the sky, an immense lattice defined by high lava walls was to emerge, following the contours and varying subtly in color and contrasts. The lava rock walls were occasionally stained with oxide paints—rust, pale green, pale blue—and sometimes painted bright solid pink. In places water was made to run along the wall tops and allowed to seep through the pores to accelerate the growth of moss. The surrounding somber mountains and the rising wilderness, juxtaposed with geometry's logic, lent to these creations the aura of inexorability which classical myths once possessed. It was as if Nature and Man's creations joined in an atavistic chant, monodic on first hearing, but which slowly began to reveal its richly intricate chromatic structure and subordinated differences of tone.

In order not to compete with or spoil this landscape's singular beauty, Barragán's house construction code had recommended simple architectural forms, abstract in quality—preferably straight lines, flat surfaces, and primary geometric volumes. As in Arcadia, the houses were not to be seen. The first house of El Pedregal was built around 1945. By 1950 there were approximately fifty houses built, but of these, Barragán would not have approved of more than six. Pressured by the subdivision's gradual but increasing success, and by the need to obtain more financing, Barragán had to relinquish enforcing his code. By 1960 El Pedregal had grown to more than 2,500 acres, with more than 900 houses built, in most cases without respect for the founder's vision. Paradise, once more, was lost.

House for Mr. Eduardo Prieto Lopez
Parque Residencial Jardines del Pedregal de San Angel,
San Angel, D.F. (pages 28–31)

House for Luis Barragán
Tacubaya, Mexico, D.F. 1947

Barragán's home is garden and house, made inextricably one. The house presents no memorable façade, joining rank, by its purposeful modesty, with the neighboring working-people's homes. It is, practically, a blank façade, its only feature a large window Barragán has, over the years, partly walled off, so that from the inside only the sky can now be seen.

The house's architectural vocabulary owes little to the international style of modern architecture. It represents a most subtle elaboration of that part of Mexico's provincial architecture Barragán loves so much: its ranches, villages, and convents. The house is divided into two levels, with a vast double-height living-room space, articulated by low walls which do not reach the ceiling (page 41). These wall-partitions create carefully studied transitions from areas of profound shadow to contrasting zones of diffused, gentle lighting. The closely beamed ceiling emphasizes the vanishing of perspective lines, reinforcing the perception of the ceiling as a detached horizontal plane, hovering high above the living areas. Space flows majestically like liquid silence, seeming to spill over the edge of the mezzanine's high parapet. The suggestion of unseen presences dwelling behind this mezzanine wall is irresistible. A very graceful stairway of cantilevered pine boards leads to a door that is always closed, and although the stair is very sturdy, its visual delicacy is such that to ascend it would seem possible only if gradual weightlessness was achieved (page 39). This stairway is a delightful elaboration of one depicted in Jan Vredeman de Vries's book *Perspective*, published in Leiden in 1604–05, and of which contemporary facsimiles abound. Like many other admirers of Surrealism, Barragán must have been fascinated by the dream-like quality of Vredeman's drawings of solitary architectural spaces.

Rudimentary elements are sensitively used throughout the house to achieve a subdued visual drama. Materials are left in their near-natural state: roughly plastered walls and volcanic rock tiles are juxtaposed with polished wooden floors, homespuns, and velvety carpets. An air of noble austerity pervades the house; the only instance of visible pride is the extraordinary quality of the Mexican ceramics, textiles, and wood carvings adorning it.

Facing the garden, at the other end of the living room, is the largest window, its glass divided into four panes by cruciform mullions, but set flush in the walls, floor and ceiling (page 40). The garden enters the house through this window like an evanescent tide of light and color. The dining table is nearby, placed inside the house during the rainy season, and outside on a pink brick uncovered terrace during the rest of the year. The garden is enclosed by high walls on three sides; the fourth side is defined by the rear façade of the house. All rooms look into the garden. When Barragán moved into the house, the lawn was formal and kept impeccably clipped. Now, he has allowed it to return to a controlled form of wilderness.

Barragán's masterful control of planes is superbly evidenced in the strong walls of the highly abstract roof terrace (pages 35–37, 42–43). Like the garden, the terrace has also undergone changes over the years. When first built the walls were all roughly plastered in white. In later years, Barragán had one of the walls painted red, and another an earthy brown. The intense Mexican sun consumes all colors, and, like a ritual, the walls must be periodically repainted. Also, at first, the roof terrace had a low, open wooden railing, facing the garden. After a number of years Barragán had it rebuilt, as a solid wooden parapet. Years later still, this wooden parapet was replaced by a wall as high as all the others surrounding it. The terrace, once open onto the garden, became an enclosed patio, framing the view onto the sky. The house now communes with two gardens, one made of leaves and passing birds, the other of winds and migrant clouds.

Chapel for the Capuchinas Sacramentarias del Purísimo Corazón de Maria
Tlalpan, Mexico, D.F. 1952–1955

Barragán has always admired the beatific figure of St. Francis, his cult of Nature and Beauty, and the innumerable expressions of religious art he inspired. Over a period of three years, Barragán designed and built, and then bequeathed to a Franciscan order of nuns, a chapel and a garden, located in Tlalpan, near Mexico City. Las Capuchinas Sacramentarias del Purísimo Corazón de Maria is one of the most cloistered orders of the Catholic Church. The sisters never leave the convent, praying forgiveness for the world's sins.

The chapel's walls are roughly textured, painted in a luminous lemon color; the floors, of large wooden planks, release a honey-colored glow. The chapel is pervaded by a delicately warm light, which fills its space with an air of radiance (page 47). Light enters from two sources which filter and transform it. Natural, but softened, light enters the rear of the chapel through a concrete lattice wall painted yellow. More-accented light comes in through a golden glass window designed by sculptor Mathias Goeritz. This light source, hidden from view, illuminates the large wooden cross from the side, projecting a cruciform shadow on the altar (page 48). The altar itself is a simple slab which supports a revered image, backdropped by a gold-leafed triptych, also designed by Mathias Goeritz. The triptych, devoid of imagery, reflects the light coming through the golden window as well as the flickering lights of the altar candles (page 49).

Using but a few rich, tactile materials and light, Barragán creates a strongly mystical ambience. The wealth of Barragán's restraint is nowhere more dazzling than in the plain wooden lattice which separates the main chapel from the small one where the novices pray (page 50). There the ceiling is lower, and stops before reaching the main chapel's wall to allow the descent of filtered light from above. This light cascades between the wooden lattice and a free-standing screen, which seems almost diaphonous as the flood of light surrounds it (page 51). The light filtering through the lattice into the main chapel illuminates it with a halo.

In the patio, purple bougainvillea tumble down the walls. A black stone fountain is used for preparing flowers for the altar (page 52). Water, lying like a mirror, stretches to the brim. With great simplicity, the patio is turned into the sky's façade. Alongside the fountain a cement lattice wall is painted a pale yellow on the outside, and on the inside, a brighter yellow, which even on cloudy days throws a pattern of sun-like light on the inner corridor (page 53). Throughout the secluded convent, sun is the ineffable presence. St. Francis must be pleased.

The Towers of Satellite City

Queretaro Highway, Mexico City. 1957,
in collaboration with Mathias Goeritz

These five large abstract Towers, created to serve as promotional symbols identifying the large residential subdivision of Ciudad Satellite, have also assumed the role of sentinels at Mexico City's northern entrance.

When Barragán was commissioned to study this project he invited Mathias Goeritz, who had previously worked with him, to collaborate. Barragán and Goeritz had each, on his own, anticipated the images which were to crystallize in the Towers. Barragán's previous work reveals an aesthetic preference for abstract prismatic qualities. Goeritz had, in earlier sculptures, searched for the emotional qualities such tall forms evoke. Over the years both had shared many ideas about art and life. But what brought them together may have been the similarly intense passion both feel for very opposing goals: while Barragán searches for Apollo, Goeritz invokes Dionysus.

The Towers stand 100, 120, 130, 150, and 165 feet high on a flat plateau, counterpointing the distant hills which surround the city, their bright colors visible from a great distance. They were built, foot by foot, almost without scaffolding, sprouting of themselves, as it were, using metal molds which climbed one upon the other until complete. The signs of this form of growth can be seen in the horizontal stripes which modulate and visually enhance the towers' height. The land on which they stand is sloped; aided by their triangular plan these shafts seem to navigate their sharp keels in a forward motion. As the viewer moves around, they seem constantly to shift profiles and change heights. From one viewpoint they appear as planar sheets; from another they resemble square-based towers. The clouds which promenade the vast flatness of Mexico City's Valley seem to move slower when framed by them, as if they had entered a denser field.

Las Arboledas, residential subdivision,
suburbs of Mexico City. 1958–1961

The land on which Las Arboledas stands was once a ranch that Barragán, with a few partners, bought and subdivided. The *raison d'être* of this project, and of others which were to follow, was the horse. The residents were expected to be, first of all, horsemen. Barragán designed the streets, established building norms and created all public gardens and fountains. Special paths for horses and gathering places for riders were delineated. The French Riding School came to establish itself here. For the School, Barragán created a series of walled enclosures, watering troughs, fountains and pools, all around and through a majestic avenue of eucalyptus trees, once the ranch's main approach.

At the entrance to the subdivision, Barragán built a red stucco wall over 100 yards long, purposefully bent at the middle to emphasize its disappearance over the horizon. The uniformity of the stucco wall and the tension of its length confer upon it the quality of a minimal sculpture, emphasized by the small scale of the traffic island's brick pavement. This red wall, at first designed to hide the subdivision from the visitor's view, is also his introduction to the mysteries of the place (pages 70–71).

Flanking the processional avenue of eucalyptus is the Plaza del Campanario (Plaza of the Bell). Here water is a continuous presence, its sound murmuring along the riders' path. Large trees, and a palisade of pinkish saplings, define the fountain's backdrop. A rectangular water tank, shoulder height, rests on a mirror of water. The tension of the water's weight pressing against the tank's walls and threatening to over-flow is relieved by a corner spout through which water cascades (page 65).

Not far away, at the culmination of the eucalyptus avenue, is the Plaza y Fuente del Bebedero (Plaza and Fountain of the Trough, pages 66–67). A ponderous stillness seems to dwell among the trees, while the shadows of branches are silhouetted across a tall free-standing white wall (pages 68–69). Magritte meets here the Persian garden-makers. Magritte would have appreciated its Surrealist qualities; the Persians would have admired the many meanings water assumes in Barragán's austere ensemble. The Persians would have also recognized in Barragán a kindred spirit for his handling of the raised, brimful trough, the hidden water outlets, and the narrow drip gutter—a device they also knew for obtaining a solid reflecting image without surface ripples or edge interruptions. The length of the trough is masterfully scaled to emphasize the avenue's long axis. It is difficult to resist imagining a horse slowly trotting down the avenue, its innocence the only power to break the enchantment and turn liquid the solid mirror.

Los Clubes, residential subdivision,
suburb of Mexico City. 1963–1964

This time his own client, Barragán was able to enforce successfully the equestrian character he wanted to give this residential subdivision. As a symbol, he designed a heroically scaled fountain for horses, Fuente de Los Clubes, or Fuente de los Amantes (Lovers' Fountain, as the two derelict horse troughs became known, pages 78–79). A long pink stucco wall assumes here the role of an abstract frieze against which the profiles of approaching horsemen turn into dynamic bas reliefs (pages 74–75). On one side, two walls meet to create an echo chamber where hoofbeats mark a rhythm against the water's gushing *basso continuo.* A red-earth stuccoed wall emerges from the pool to shoulder an aqueduct carrying water (pages 76–77 and 82–83), which originates, perhaps, in Barragán's childhood memories.

The magic play of shadows and reflections against solid and liquid surfaces achieves in this fountain lyric perfection. There is an enchanted moment of the day when all walls seem to stop casting their own shadows so that the aqueduct can silhouette itself as a straight shadow line against the gushing water. De Chirico, Delvaux, and Magritte must always have known that this fountain existed. A place where cobblestones seem to melt into water the sun will later turn into clouds (pages 80–81).

Like Mies's Barcelona Pavilion, this composition achieves a superior sense of balance by dynamically counterpoising visual elements, rather than by resorting to formal symmetries. The luminous effect is one of classic serenity and mythological beauty —a pagan temple for the communion of horse with rider.

Porton de Servicio (Service Gate),
Los Clubes. 1968–1969

Through this gate the riders return from their excursions. A carpet of small bricks, carefully laid out to emphasize perspective, forms a ramp that rises from the outside road and once past the gate slowly begins to descend. A free-standing wall protects the flank, opposite the gatekeeper's room which has tiny lookout windows reinforcing its fortress-like quality. The wooden gates are hinged in such a manner that once folded they also stand as isolated planes. Only when riders parade through this gate, framed by wall and cubic volume, is Barragán's Paolo Uccello-like composition fulfilled.

San Cristobal, stable, horse pool, swimming pool
and house for Mr. and Mrs. Folke Egerstrom,
subdivision Los Clubes, suburb of Mexico, D.F. 1967–1968,
with the collaboration of architect Andrés Casillas

This work completes what may be seen as Barragán's equestrian trilogy: the processional avenue, the temple, and, now, the academy. Mr. and Mrs. Folke Egerstrom, the owners of this unique stable, breed thoroughbreds they train as race horses. Before being taken to run in an adjoining field, the horses are exercised within an enclosure defined by box stalls, pink and red-rust colored walls, and a great flat water pool. The walls are designed to the scale of a horse. Under the sun, reflected in the pool and enveloped by silence, these hieratical walls acquire a legendary significance (pages 92–94). In this setting the horse is the Actor, leaving and entering through two masterful openings cut in a long pink wall, while riders enter plainly from the house, and grooms filter in between a double layer of purple walls (pages 94–95).

The stone paving in front of the box stalls ramps down gently to create the pool's basin. The pool is fed by water gushing through an edge of the red-rust colored wall (page 96). This wall also serves to shield visually the stable wing from one of the entrance doors. Barragán manages, with this one wall, to introduce with lyric effortlessness two aspects of high ritual: the suggestion of a space beyond, and, even more magically, transubstantiation. The alchemistic vision of all Surrealists is here proven true: solid matter has a liquid core. As we round the edge of the wall, we discover that the solid wall is in reality a double plane with water running in between (page 101). This ambivalence is further contrasted when it is observed that it is only this corner which has begun to liquefy—at the other end the wall still remains solid, as a door-window cut through it makes evident. The second pink wall, higher, and modulated by two slot-like cuts to reveal its planar properties, seems to suggest a fortification (page 97). But like many other military constructions this one is also camouflage, for it hides the haystack.

The Egerstrom house is formally conceived as a multi-layered series of planes of different height defining a volume. One of its most accomplished features is the double wall which shields a long open corridor leading toward one of the entrances (page 100). The swimming pool with steps descending into the water is partly covered by a baldachino-like structure (page 102), echoing an 18th-century arcaded pavilion left windowless and surrounded on three sides by water when Empress Carlota had the Borda gardens rebuilt in Cuernavaca.

The Egerstrom house is Barragán's most complex creation. With extraordinary discipline and very few architectural elements he has recreated a micro-model of the *pueblos* he knew as a child: the house, the plaza, the horses, the friendly trees, and the water coming from very far away. Twenty years separate this house from the one Barragán designed for himself in the Tacubaya section of Mexico City, but it is evident that both were designed for the same person. Like Borges, Barragán is the author of one archetypal story inexhaustibly reformulated. If the story is a private one, the artistry it expresses belongs to our heritage of great architectural poetry.

Luis Barragán

An engineer by training, Barragán is an autodidactic architect who learned the profession by direct experience and through the works of artist friends and architectural writers. An important local influence was Jesus "Chucho" Reyes, a "naive" primitive painter whose philosophy toward life and art Barragán has shared, being bound by the same loyalties to their native *pueblo* of Guadalajara. Barragán also generously acknowledges the philosophical influence of Mathias Goeritz, the German-born sculptor who, since the late 40s, has been working and teaching in Mexico. Barragán is also fond of recalling as an influence the house and the personalities of Rosa and Miguel Covarrubias, photographer and scholar, respectively, who for decades acted as the unofficial curators of Mexican culture. But the most decisive influence in Barragán's work has been the popular architecture of Mexico's villages, ranches and convents.

His family owned ranches in the State of Jalisco, in whose small towns he spent his youth, riding horses, attending fiestas, and visiting market places. He came to Mexico City for the first time in his early twenties in transit to Europe. It was during this trip that he discovered the writings of Ferdinand Bac, a French intellectual, painter and landscape architect, whom he came to meet only later, in 1931, during another trip to France. Bac's influence upon Barragán was more one of attitude than of form, but his philosophic and poetic images conjured up for Barragán a vision that never left him: the garden as a magic place for the enjoyment of meditation and companionship.

In 1924 he visited the beautiful gardens of La Alhambra in Spain. The enchanted progression of its brilliantly composed spaces, fountains, and water channels have had a lasting effect on his work. It is from the Islamic notion of compartmentalized and successive garden spaces that Barragán developed his feeling for walled enclosures and his love for the sound of running water. Another influence on his work has been the Moorish architecture of North Africa, especially Morocco. Although he did not visit North Africa until 1951, he had long cherished images of its houses and mosques in the travel and architecture books he brought back from his first European sojourn. His fascination with Moorish architecture was paid homage in several early houses he built in Guadalajara (houses for González Luna and Enrique Aguilar, page 112). Since then, Barragán's mind has remained attuned to the intimate garden. Although he prefers the Italian baroque to the courtly French, it is the sensual intimacy of the Islamic garden which seduces him. Barragán's gardens, or rather his open-enclosures, are endowed with erotic and metaphysical properties; they are places for the pleasures of the senses and the mind, bewitched regions leading to fantastic dreams and fable making. In this regard, it must be noticed that Barragán has never created large public plazas in populated areas, with the exception of a kindergarten in Guadalajara (children's playground, page 113), which by its nature had to be enclosed. Only once did he attempt to design a large public space, in the never realized project for Plaza de la Constitución or El Zócalo, as Mexico City's main plaza is called. His proposal shows a secluded, below-ground-level space containing an enclosed water fountain (La Plaza del Zócalo, page 119) leaving the large, raised plaza level barren of anything but the elegant traces of a de Chirico-like grid.

Barragán has always endeavored to create an architectural language which would express man's eternal longings in the context of modern Mexico's natural and cultural conditions. Shunning the use of familiar Mexican forms, the character of his architecture results from its continuity with Mexico's splendid architectural traditions.

Barragán acknowledges his love for and aesthetic debt to the popular architecture of Mexico's ranches, villages and convents. But it should be noted that Mexico's climate and natural resources have always been strong factors in the formal development of its architecture. The incandescent luminosity of its sun, the strong winds and heavy rains, and the restrictions of poverty and unskilled labor have all contributed to a discipline of structural simplicity and few materials. Mexico's popular and cosmopolitan architectures have both responded to their physical milieu with similarly introspective attitudes, creating enclosed forms with interior worlds of patios and secluded gardens. The formal properties of this architecture involve the interplay of positive and negative volumes: masses and voids. In this tradition the void plays several roles; it is the vessel for light and shadow, and it also serves as the compositional nexus binding the different masses. Barragán's architecture recognizes similar roles for the void, but assigns it stronger dynamic properties by dematerializing some of the surfaces defining its edges. In a process of further abstraction, Barragán's masses are condensed into planes. Thus a part comes to stand for the whole; the wall becomes the surrogate for the rooms which once surrounded the patio, and the life these rooms once housed—a child playing on the floor, a woman pedaling on her sewing machine, the smoke of darkened kitchens—seem now to dwell as unseen presences behind these walls.

Barragán is the outstanding exponent of an architectural tradition which the modern movement has neglected: stage architecture. His compositions possess background, middleground and foreground; monumental in quality, they are deliberately static in feeling. The element of tension is always introduced by the user, whether man or horse, or more subtly, by his absence. An influence having direct bearing on this aspect of Barragán's architecture are the 17th and 18th century *atrios* of Mexico's unique "open-air churches," designed to receive the thousands of new native converts attending mass. The church's façade assumed, from the atrium, the quality of a miraculous shield, behind which the divine powers dwelled. It was an image of God's house the natives could easily associate with their previous religious experience.

The extraordinary emotional effect of Barragán's compositions and the strong sensual qualities of his materials and colors cannot be guessed from his drawings or plans. The architectural richness of Barragán's dramatically sober architecture is based on a few constructive elements bound together by a mystical feeling, an austerity exalted by the glory of his brilliant colors. They pervade all the interstices of space, at once binding and separating artifact and nature. Paint is for him like a garment the wall puts on to relate to its surroundings. Under the bright Mexican light the splendor of the color lasts but an instant; the sun ravages it as the seasons change, and, soon, when the leaves return, a new coat is needed. Intimately bound to Barragán's sensitivity for color is his animistic feeling for matter. He seems to endow matter with a soul of its own. In his work, the wall is assumed to possess a skin and a core; it breathes and palpitates, like an animal. If a wall is punctured, the wedge turns into a spigot through which the wall slowly drips. Whenever a wall is split open, it reveals its liquid core (page 101). As in Surrealist painting, Barragán's walls have two sides. One, open and direct, which the viewer faces. The other, shrouded in shadows, suggests past presences. As for the users of these fabulous landscapes, their roles are carefully formalized. Only horses can walk through wall openings. Man may only filter in between wall planes (pages 94–95). The exceptions are children and riders.

Barragán's creative instincts lead him to action rather than to polemics. Leaving aside theoretical scaffoldings, Barragán works within the constraints of a frugal formal vocabulary. His architecture results from an almost redemptive commitment to beauty. Since he does not follow theoretical rules or generalized systems, each project is an entity in itself, whose inner principles must be revealed. This procedure demands emotional sensibility and selective intuition. Like Mies van der Rohe, Barragán deals only with the inner tensions of each element. This has led him to concise and profound creations, hard to surpass.

It is a lonely road but, as he confesses, it is only among architects that he feels himself to be the stranger. Not for any anti-intellectual bias, but because he believes their education has estranged them from their own emotional and intuitive capacities. Barragán's aesthetic preferences, and the monumental sense of his compositions have, occasionally, been perceived as scenographic and socially uncommitted. But Barragán's concerns, while paying their dues to function, go beyond the requirements of a program of utilitarian needs to satisfy the necessities of what may be called *a program of metaphysical imperatives*. In a culture exhausted and irreparably fragmented, the walls surrounding Barragán's gardens are, perhaps, one of the last defenses to preserve centuries of thought and emotion. If after the Revolution there will be Serenity, Barragán's architecture will surely provide one of its models.

All of Barragán's projects are autobiographical; or so they became, as in the case of the gardens of El Pedregal. His sympathy for Surrealism stems from perceiving it as an existential attitude with a romantic undertone he relates to longing (in one of Barragán's favorite books *The Unquiet Grave* by Cyril Connolly, one can find underlined the following passage: "Art is memory's *mise-en-scène*."). He believes, with Connolly, that "art is made by the alone for the alone."

In Mexico the past is always present, and its architecture is charged with ancestral presences. Death is its central tragedy and its ever present memory. Catholic resignation is the silent chorus, the core of its passion and humbleness. A stoical acceptance of solitude as man's fate permeates Barragán's work. In the settings of his magnificent plazas, man can take communion with his solitude. And also take pleasure in it, Barragán would add, for, as a devout Catholic, he believes that man's condition is God's will, and must, therefore, be accepted with dignity and love.

Barragán's solitude is cosmic; Mexico is the temporal abode he lovingly accepts. It is for the greater glory of this House that he has created gardens where Man can make peace with himself, and a chapel where his passions and desires may be forgiven and his faith proclaimed. One complements the other. The garden is the myth of the Beginning and the chapel that of the End. For Barragán, House is the form Man gives to his life between both extremes.   —Emilio Ambasz

Period 1927 to 1936

The houses Barragán designed in this period, before leaving his native Guadalajara for Mexico City, reflect his fascination with Moslem architecture, especially that of Morocco; these patios and gardens are Barragán's romantic evocation of Mediterranean terraces.

House restoration for Mr. Robles León, Guadalajara, State of Jalisco, 1927.

Rental houses for Mr. Robles León, Guadalajara, State of Jalisco, 1928.

House for Mrs. Harper de Garibi, Guadalajara, State of Jalisco, 1928.

House for Mr. E. González Luna, Guadalajara,
State of Jalisco, 1928.

House for Mr. Enrique Aguilar, Guadalajara,
State of Jalisco, 1928.

House for Mr. G. Cristo, Guadalajara,
State of Jalisco, 1929.

Children's playground in the Parque de la Revolución, Guadalajara, State of Jalisco, 1929.

Two rental houses, property of Mr. E. González Luna, Guadalajara, State of Jalisco, 1929.

House restoration for the Barragán family, Chapala, State of Jalisco, 1931.

House restoration, Guadalajara, State of Jalisco, 1932, in collaboration with engineer Juan Palomar.

Period 1936 to 1940

The projects of this period, designed for Mexico City, evidence the influence of the International Style in architecture, especially Le Corbusier's work. Carefully composed and meticulously detailed, they already contain the germs of Barragán's later conceptions, as revealed, for example, by his treatment of the buildings' façades. Remarkable among these projects is the apartment building on Plaza Melchor Ocampo for the manner in which Barragán bends the façade to emphasize its planar quality, and the delicacy with which the balconies are cut out to suggest transparency.

House for two families in Avenida Parque Mexico,
Mexico, D.F., 1936.

Two rental houses, in Avenida Mazatlán,
Mexico, D.F., 1936.

House for Mr. I. Pizarro Suárez, Las Lomas de Chapultepec,
Mexico, D.F., 1937.

Apartment building on the corner of Calles Lerma
y Guadiana, Mexico, D.F., 1936–40.

Rental house on Calle Guadiana, Mexico, D.F., 1936–40.

Apartment building on Avenida Mississippi,
Mexico, D.F., 1936–40.

Apartment building on Plaza Melchor Ocampo,
Mexico, D.F., 1936–40, in collaboration with
architect José Creixell.

Apartment building with adjoining single house on
Avenida Mississippi, Mexico, D.F., 1936–40.

Building composed of four painters' studios on Plaza
Melchor Ocampo, Mexico, D.F., 1936–40.

Three low-cost apartment buildings on Calle de Elba,
Mexico, D.F., 1936–40.

Four private gardens on Avenida Constituyentes y Calle General Francisco Ramírez, Mexico, D.F.

During this period Barragán created four contiguous private gardens on a property he owned in the Tacubaya section of Mexico City. One of those gardens formed part of a house he reconstructed and lived in until it was later sold (illustrated, right). The other two were also sold for residential use. The fourth garden became part of the house he built for himself and where he presently lives (pages 33–43).

This early garden already reveals Barragán's emphasis on the use of planes, not vertical, as those he utilized in later work, but horizontal, defining three terraces connected by stone retaining walls. Without using high walls, Barragán achieves a feeling of enclosed garden space by means of an open composition of multilevered planes which suggest an ever more intimate feeling the further the visitor descends toward the pool.

Three private gardens on the Avenida San Jerónimo in San Angel, D.F., on land contiguous to El Pedregal de San Angel, D.F.

In 1944 Barragán bought a piece of land, called El Cabrío, on the outer edges of what was later to become the subdivision of El Pedregal. His intention in acquiring El Cabrío was to create a series of enclosed garden spaces where he could retire from time to time to meditate and enjoy nature. In designing these gardens Barragán took advantage of the marvelous terrain and big evergreen oaks, using the water of the bordering river to feed pools and artificial waterfalls. Nowhere in his other work has Barragán's imagery resembled so closely that of the Surrealist painters and film makers than in these gardens.

House for Mr. Eduardo Villaseñor, San Angel, D.F., 1940.

El Pedregal (The Rocky Place), formally known as Parque Residencial Jardines del Pedregal de San Angel, periphery of Mexico, D.F., 1945–50 (pages 11–27).

Barragán subdivided this volcanic area into suburban plots, also designing the road system, the water supply layout, and all works of public landscaping and ornamentation.

His designs for El Pedregal consisted among others of three demonstration gardens, one of which features the Fuente de los Patos (Fountain of the Ducks, page 20), a pond among the lava rocks (page 21), and several walkways among the rocks (pages 16–19). He also designed the Plaza de las Fuentes (Plaza of the Fountains) which functions as one of the entrances to El Pedregal, featuring a water jet fountain (page 13), a sculpture by Mathias Goeritz, railings and tree groupings. A second entrance to El Pedregal designed by Barragán comprised an iron gate painted in phosphorescent colors and a red metal road-circle to organize vehicular circulation (pages 22–23). Another entrance, mainly used for service vehicles, consisted of two combs of vertical iron bars, which open by rotating on their middle points (pages 24–25).

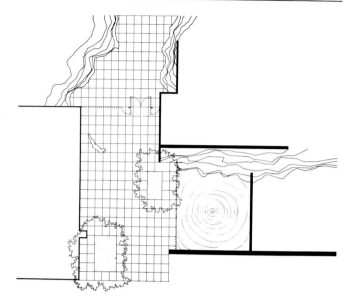

House for Luis Barragán, Tacubaya, Mexico, D.F., 1947 (pages 33–43).

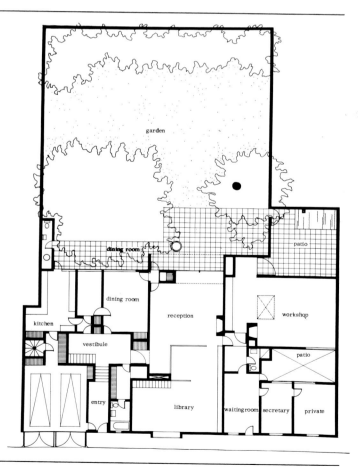

Plaza del Cigarro (Cigar Plaza), Parque Residencial
Jardines del Pedregal de San Angel, San Angel, D.F.

Designed to function as a water tank, the central element of
this plaza was not built as per Barragán's recommendations.
The platform on which the cylindrical water tank rests has
become occupied in later years by unrelated constructions.

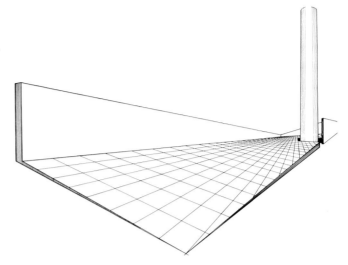

House for Mr. Eduardo Prieto Lopez, Parque Residencial
Jardines del Pedregal de San Angel, San Angel, D.F.
(pages 28–31).

Two houses, Avenida de las Fuentes 10 and 12,
Parque Residencial Jardines del Pedregal de San Angel,
San Angel, D.F., 1948. Max Cetto, architect, with the
collaboration of Luis Barragán.

Chapel for the Capuchinas Sacramentarias del Purísimo Corazón de Maria, and restoration of their existing convent, Tlalpan, D.F., 1952–55 (pages 45–53).

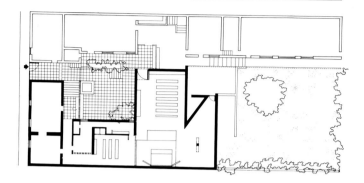

La Plaza del Zócalo, study for fountain and mall for Plaza de la Constitución, also known as El Zócalo, Mexico, D.F., 1953.

Gardens for the Hotel Pierre Marquez, Acapulco, State of Guerrero, 1955.

Barragán designed only the gardens of this hotel, planning the location of the entrance, parking lot, swimming pool, stables, lake, and tennis court.

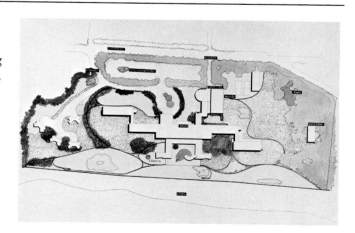

House for Mr. Antonio Galvez, Calle Pimentel 10,
San Angel, D.F., 1955.

Jardines del Bosque, master plan for subdivision,
Guadalajara, State of Jalisco, 1955.

Capilla del Calvario, design of chapel for subdivision
Jardines del Bosque (not built), Guadalajara,
State of Jalisco, 1955.

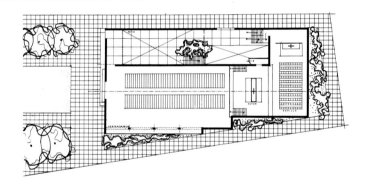

Towers of Satellite City, Queretaro Highway,
Mexico, D.F., 1957, in collaboration with
Mathias Goeritz (pages 55–61).

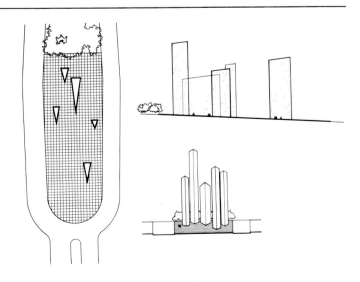

Las Arboledas, master plan and building code for residential subdivision, suburbs of Mexico City, 1958–61 (pages 63–71).

In addition to the master plan, Barragán designed for this subdivision El Muro Rojo (The Red Wall), 1958 (pages 70–71) the Plaza del Campanario (Plaza of the Bell), 1959 (plan top right, illustrated page 65), and the Plaza y Fuente del Bebedero (Plaza and Fountain of the Trough), 1959 (plan bottom right, illustrated pages 66–69).

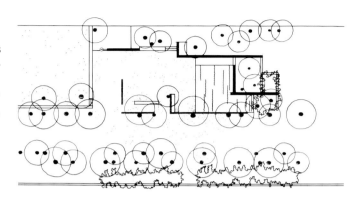

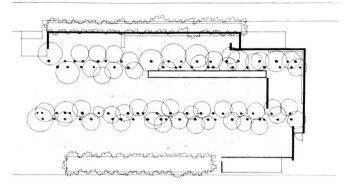

Los Clubes, master plan, public landscaping, and building code for residential subdivision, suburbs of Mexico City, 1963–64 (pages 73–89).

Barragán designed for this subdivision the Fuente de Los Clubes, also known as Fuente de los Amantes (Lovers' Fountain), utilizing two derelict troughs placed on their ends in the foreground. Later, in 1968, Barragán designed a service entrance (pages 86–89).

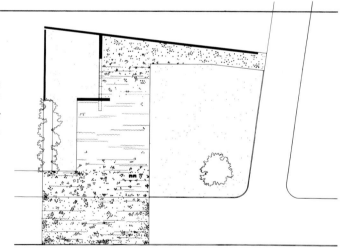

Lomas Verdes, master plan for residential subdivision, composed of twenty thousand dwelling units, draft of building code and design of "symbol" building, 1964–67, in partnership with architect Juan Sordo Madaleno.

Design of open Chapel for Lomas Verdes, 1964–67.

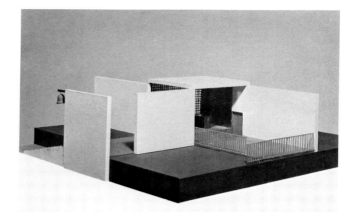

San Cristobal, stable, horse pool, swimming pool and house for Mr. and Mrs. Folke Egerstrom, subdivision Los Clubes, suburb of Mexico, D.F., 1967–68, with the collaboration of architect Andrés Casillas (pages 91–103).

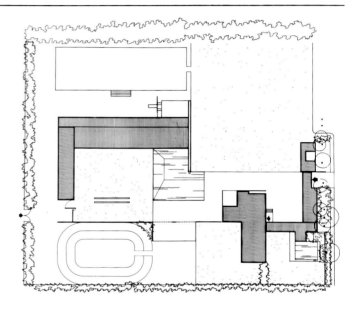

Cano, master plan and entrance to subdivision, near Tepotzotlan, 1969.

Preliminary design for a club and race track,
subdivision, Guadalajara, State of Jalisco, 1971.

Monumental fountain for Lomas Verdes (not yet built),
1972, in collaboration with architect Ricardo Legorreta.

The water of this fountain cascades from a 75-foot horizontal cantilever onto an inclined plane, draining into a canal which carries the water to be recycled.

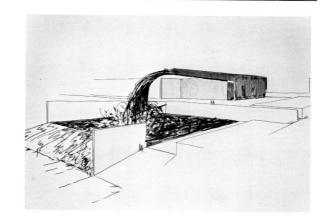

Preliminary design of a 165-foot symbolic tower to house
pigeons in the residential subdivision, El Palomar,
a suburb of Guadalajara, State of Jalisco, 1973,
with the collaboration of architect Raul Ferrera.

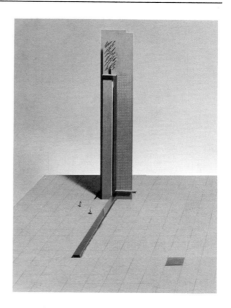

House for Mr. Gilardi, Tacubaya section of Mexico City,
construction to start spring, 1976.

Designed as a residence for a small family on a plot of land 30 feet wide and 100 feet deep, surrounded by buildings on three sides. Great attention has been given to the design of a covered pool which, in addition to serving as a swimming pool, will have alongside it an area for lounging which can also be used for dining.

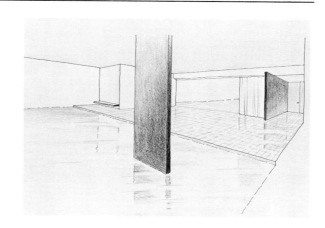

Bibliography

Since many of the articles are unsigned the periodicals listing has been organized chronologically; where we have an author's name it has been included. Barragán's work is discussed in a number of books, and these are listed alphabetically by author for convenience.

Books

Born, Esther. *The New Architecture in Mexico*. New York, The Architectural Record, W. Morrow & Company, 1937.

Cetto, Max L. *Moderne Architektur in Mexiko*. Teufen, A. Niggli, [1961].

Futagawa, Yukio. *Global Interior #2, "Latin America."* Tokyo, A.D.A. EDITA, undated.

Hitchcock, Henry-Russell. *Latin American Architecture Since 1945*. New York, The Museum of Modern Art, 1955.

Kassler, Elizabeth B. *Modern Gardens and the Landscape*. New York, The Museum of Modern Art, 1964.

Kirby, Rosina Greene. *Mexican Landscape Architecture—From the Street and from Within*. Tucson, The University of Arizona Press, 1972.

Laos, Hernandez. *Analisis Critico de la Arquitectura Moderna en Mexico*. Guadalajara, Escuela de Arquitectura Universidad de Guadalajara, 1968.

Myers, I.E. in cooperation with the National Institute of Fine Arts of Mexico. *Mexico's Modern Architecture*. New York, Architectural Book Publishing Co., 1952.

Redstone, Louis G. *Art in Architecture*. New York, McGraw-Hill Book Company, 1968.

Rodman, Selden. *Mexican Journal: The Conquerors Conquered*. New York, The Devin-Adair Co., 1958.

Shipway, Verna Cook and Warren. *Mexican Homes of Today*. New York, Architectural Book Publishing Co., [1964].

Smith, Clive Bamford. *Builders in the Sun: Five Mexican Architects*. New York, Architectural Book Publishing Co., 1967.

Yáñez, Enrique. *18 Residencias de Arquitectos Mexicanos*. Mexico, Ediciones Mexicanas, 1951.

Periodicals

"Mexican Villas: Luis Barragán, Architect." *Architectural Record* (New York), September, 1931, pp. 162–164. House for Mr. G. R. Cristo in Guadalajara.

"Modernist Houses in Mexico Designed by Luis Barragán." *House & Garden* (New York), October, 1931, pp. 56–57. Houses for Messrs. Enrique Aguilar, E. González Luna, Robles León, I. Franco and G. R. Cristo in Guadalajara.

"Carpeta de Arquitectura Mejicana." *Nuestra Arquitectura* (Buenos Aires), March, 1932, pp. 323–330. Houses for Messrs. G. R. Cristo, Efrain González Luna, Enrique Aguilar and E. R. León in Guadalajara.

"Los Patios de Guadalajara." *Jueves de Excelsior* (Mexico, D.F.), September 15, 1932.

"Recent Work of a Mexican Architect—Luis Barragán." *Architectural Record* (New York), January, 1935, pp. 33–46. The architect's summer house renovation in Chapala; remodeled houses for Mrs. Harper de Garibi and Mr. Robles León in Guadalajara.

Domus (Milan), August, 1935, p. 27. Photo spread of the architect's summer house renovation in Chapala; houses for Mrs. Harper de Garibi and Mr. Robles León in Guadalajara.

"Parque de La Revolución, Guadalajara, Jalisco, Mexico." *Architectural Record* (New York), September, 1935, pp. 165–169. Children's playground in Guadalajara.

Architectural Record (New York), April, 1937, pp. 76–79. Speculation House and two-family house in Mexico City.

"Luis Barragán, Dos de Sus Obras." *Arquitectura y Decoracion* (Mexico City), September, 1937, pp. 31–37. Two-family house and single-family house in Mexico City.

"Edificio de Departamentos en Mexico, D.F." *Arquitectura 10* (Mexico, D.F.), July, 1942, pp. 33–36. Apartment building in Mexico City.

"Dos Jardines en Mexico, D.F., por Luis Barragán, Arq." *Arquitectura 18* (Mexico, D.F.), July, 1945, pp. 148–155. Garden in Mexico City; experimental garden in El Pedregal.

Saint Albans, Mary. "The Gardens of Pedregal." *Modern Mexico* (New York), April, 1946. pp. 10–11, 29.

"El Pedregal y Barragán." *Espacios* (Mexico, D.F.), September, 1948. Photo spread of El Pedregal.

Arquitectura y Lo Demas (Mexico City), March-December, 1948. Advertisement for Jardines del Pedregal de San Angel, S.A.

Espacios 5 y 6 (Mexico, D.F.), 1950. Barragán's house and studio in Mexico City.

"El Pedregal." *Espacios* (Mexico, D.F.), August, 1950.

"Jardines del Pedregal, Mexico City." "House by Luis Barragán, Architect." *Arts & Architecture* (Los Angeles), August, 1951, pp. 20–23, 24–25. El Pedregal, Barragán's house in Mexico City.

"Casa Habitación, Luis Barragán, Arq." *Arquitectura Mexico 35* (Mexico, D.F.), September, 1951, pp. 285–290.

"El Pedregal: Un Nuevo Paisaje de Singular y Unica Belleza." "Caminos Sobre Rocas." *Construcción Moderna* (Mexico City), November-December, 1951, pp. 66–71, 72–81.

"Habitacion en Los Jardines del Pedregal." *Espacios 8* (Mexico, D.F.), December, 1951. Houses in El Pedregal.

Crespo de la Serna, Jorge J. "Jardines en El Pedregal." *Arquitectura Mexico 37* (Mexico City), March, 1952, pp. 110–114.

Nelken, Margarita. "El Arquitecto y Paisajista Luis Barragán." *Hoy* (Mexico, D.F.), April 26, 1952, pp. 44–45.

Barragán, Luis. "Gardens For Environment—Jardines del Pedregal." *Journal of the American Institute of Architects* (Washington, D.C.), April, 1952, pp. 167–172. Address before the California Council of Architects and the Sierra Nevada Regional Conference, Coronado, California. October 6, 1951.

"Mexico, The Garden in the Stony Place." *Harper's Bazaar* (New York), June, 1952, pp. 66–67. El Pedregal.

McCoy, Esther. "House on a Lava Bed." *The New York Times Magazine* (New York), August 17, 1952, pp. 42–43. House in El Pedregal.

Architectural Forum (New York), September, 1952, pp. 102–103. El Pedregal.

"Los Jardines del Pedregal." *Arquitectura Mexico 39* (Mexico, D.F.), September, 1952, pp. 341–345.

McCoy, Esther. "Barragán's House." *Los Angeles Times Home Magazine* (Los Angeles), October 19, 1952, pp. 8–9.

"Mexico's Pedregal Gardens." *House & Home* (New York), October, 1952, pp. 126–133.

"Los Jardines del Pedregal de San Angel." *Espacios 11-12* (Mexico, D.F.), October, 1952. Photo spread on El Pedregal.

Fleisher, Horace. "The Gardens of the Pedregal—Contemporary Design in a Land Subdivision in Mexico." *Landscape Architecture* (Louisville, Kentucky), January, 1953, pp. 48–53.

Ponti, Gio. "Il Pedregal di Città del Messico." *Domus* (Milan), March, 1953, pp. 15–22.

MacDonald, Antonio Vargas. "Pedregal." *ABC* (Mexico City), No. 103, August 22, 1953, pp. 5–7.

Cetto, Max. "Bauten In Einer Lavalandschaft Mexicos." *Baukunst und Werkform* (Darmstadt, Germany), No. 1–2, 1954, pp. 37–56. Buildings in El Pedregal.

"Jardines del Pedregal." *Madame* (Mexico City), February, 1954, pp. 46–51.

"El Pedregal de San Angel." *Ingenieria y Arquitectura* (Mexico, D.F.), May-August, 1954, pp. 28–35.

Döhnert, Horst. "Arbeiten von Luis Barragán, Mexico," in "Neue Architektur In Mexico—Ein Reisebericht." *Baukunst und Werkform* (Darmstadt, Germany), November, 1954, pp. 664–669. Barragán's work in review of recent Mexican architecture.

Lukin, Maria. "Luis Barragán, Arquitecto." *Ver y Estimar* (Buenos Aires), February, 1955, pp. 9–11.

"Le Pedregal de San Angel." "Habitations Individuelles." *L'Architecture d'aujourd'hui* (Boulogne, France), April, 1955, pp. 75–77, 78–79.

"Residencia Luis Barragán." "Pedregal de Santo Angelo." *Brasil—Arquitetura Contemporánea No. 6* (Rio de Janeiro), 1955, pp. 6–9, 30–43.

Gall, Jacques and François. "L'Operation Pedregal." *Connaissance des arts* (Paris), March, 1956, pp. 60–63.

"Mexico: The Architect at Home." *Harper's Bazaar* (New York), March, 1956, pp. 186–187.

"Barragán a Città del Messico." "Luis Barragán, Casa Prieto, Città del Messico." *Domus 321* (Milan), August, 1956, pp. 1, 2–7. Architect's house in Mexico City, house for Mr. Prieto in El Pedregal.

"Satellite City." *Mexico This Month* (Mexico City), July, 1957, pp. 20–21.

Nesbit, G. "The Towers of Satellite City." *Arts & Architecture* (Los Angeles), May, 1958, pp. 22–23.

"Mexico—Gardens of the Tiger." *Time* (Latin America Edition), March 14, 1960, pp. 21–22. Development of El Pedregal.

Artes de Mexico (Mexico City), No. 36, 1961. Barragán's house, Plaza del Bebedero in subdivision Las Arboledas, the Towers of Satellite City.

Interiors (New York), December, 1961, p. 12. Stairs of Barragán's house in review of "Stairs" Exhibition. The Museum of Modern Art, New York.

Nelson, George. "The Passionate Arts." *Holiday* (Indianapolis, Indiana), October, 1962, pp. 84–89, 175, 178–179, 181. Article on Mexican art and architecture.

Foto Magazin (Munich), October, 1962. Cover: The Towers of Satellite City.

Architectura Mexico 83 (Mexico, D.F.), September, 1963. Towers of Satellite City, El Pedregal, Barragán's house.

Damaz, Paul. "Art in Latin American Architecture." *Craft Horizons* (New York), September/October, 1963; pp. 12–39, 50–51. Review of artistic and architectural activity in Latin America.

"Master Designer, Luis Barragán." *Interiors* (New York), December, 1963, pp. 84–91.

Goeritz, Mathias. "Sobre Luis Barragán." *Arquitectos de Mexico 21* (Mexico City), No. 1, 1964, pp. 19–33. Photographic review including plans.

O'Brien, George. "No Translation Needed." *The New York Times Magazine* (New York), February 9, 1964, pp. 48–49, 51. Barragán's house.